Ketogenic Diet Holiday Recipes:

50 Ketogenic Christmas Recipes For a Healthy Meal Start to Finish

By

Ashley Peters

Table of Contents

Introduction

I want to start by thanking you for purchasing the book, *"Ketogenic Diet Holiday Recipes: 50 Ketogenic Christmas Recipes For a Healthy Meal Start to Finish"* I am honored to be helping you on this journey to create delicious homemade Ketogenic holiday recipes!

It's never to early to start planning for the holidays! Ensure your festivities are stress-free this year with our Ketogenic holiday recipes.

Christmas dinner is one of the most anticipated events of the holiday, after opening presents of course. Gathering around a well-laid table with family and friends and feasting on traditional favorites, Christmas dinner is often a memorable and joyful annual occurrence.

Planning a Ketogenic Christmas dinner, holiday dinner or other large gathering isn't complicated, but the more forethought you give it the easier it will be. The key is to do as much work ahead of time as you can, so you and your guests can enjoy yourselves the day of the party.

This book contains proven recipes and tips on how you can make quick, easy holiday Ketogenic recipes. I will provide you with everything you need to know from tools, ingredients, and recipes to storage

Thanks Again For Purchasing This Book, I Hope You Enjoy It!

What is the Ketogenic Diet? (Keto Diet)

Despite the many different kinds of diets that you have no doubt heard about in your life, there is bound to be a few that are new to you. One of these in particular might be the Ketogenic Diet, also known as the Keto Diet, which is a high-fat, low-carbohydrate regimen. The theory behind the high-fat, low-carbohydrate ratio is that the body will rely on fat for energy instead of on carbohydrates, and therefore the body will become more lean as a result of having less fat stored in the body. Ideally, the Keto Diet will allow the body to go into ketosis, or a metabolic state where ketones - which are fats - are burned for energy instead of glucose - the carbohydrates. Those that follow the Keto Diet also consume just the right amount of protein that the body needs on a daily basis. Contrary to some of the other diets that are in existence, the Keto Diet does not focus on counting calories. The focus is instead centered on the fat, carbohydrate, and protein make-up of the food as well as on the weight of the portions.

But what led to the creation of the Keto Diet? Back in 1924, a Mayo Clinic doctor by the name of Russell Wilder developed the Ketogenic Diet in hopes of finding a treatment for epilepsy. Many people who suffer from epilepsy and other illnesses have reported a noticeable decrease in their symptoms after going on this diet. This practice dates back to Ancient Greece when doctors would change their patients' diets and even have them fast to force their body into starvation mode. The Ketogenic Diet is a much easier means of getting the body to go into the fasting mode without actually depriving the body of food. To this day, however, no one knows exactly why the Ketogenic Diet is so effective in helping those that suffer from epilepsy, autism, and other known illnesses.

A typical meal for someone on the Ketogenic Diet would feature the high-fat, low-carbohydrate ratio, and might include a healthy serving of a protein such as chicken, some fruit or a protein-rich vegetable, and a high-fat component, which might be butter. The high-fat component on this diet usually comes from the ingredients which go into making the food; this could include heavy cream, butter, or buttermilk, and also might feature creamy dressings such as Ranch.

Why Choose the Ketogenic Diet?

Over the years, researchers have found that there are many benefits to choosing the Ketogenic Diet. There was initial speculation that the diet would cause a cholesterol build-up in the body, therefore leading to heart disease due to the high-fat content of the foods that people on the diet could consume. However, as more and more experts have looked into the diet, they have found that there are inherent advantages for beginning this type of diet. For one, the body is able to utilize fat instead of carbohydrates for energy. The body will therefore not rely on carbohydrates since there is such a low amount entering the body, and will thus be able to store ketones - the fats - for later energy use.

Another benefit is the fact that the body will not be as hungry, and people on the Keto Diet therefore are at a lower risk of falling off their regiment by snacking. Because the Keto Diet encourages the consumption of various protein-rich foods which work to curb hunger. The body goes into the state of ketosis - which is common among those who fast regularly - and therefore does not require a lot of food to keep it going. What better than to be on a healthy diet and not have constant hunger pangs?

Finally, the health benefits offered by the Keto Diet are remarkable. People who follow the Keto Diet completely eliminate starchy carbohydrates, such as breads and pastas, and substitute them with non-starch vegetables such as broccoli, asparagus, carrots, and many others. These kinds of vegetables are packed with vitamins and nutrients that support a healthy body, and are also much lower in calories. The Keto Diet, in addition to aiding those who suffer from illnesses such as epilepsy, is also recommended for cancer patients. As research has shown, cancer cells flourish in areas of the body where there is a lot of glucose, which is what carbohydrates become. If the body consumes less carbohydrates, there will therefore be less glucose, and subsequently the cancer cells will not be able to grow and thrive.

Benefits Of A Keto Diet

•Cholesterol. A Keto diet has shown to improve triglyceride levels and cholesterol levels most associated with arterial buildup.
•Weight Loss. As your body is burning fat as the main source of energy, you will essentially be using your fat stores as an energy source while in a fasting state.
•Blood Sugar. Many studies show the decrease of LDL cholesterol over time and have shown to eliminate ailments such as type 2 diabetes.
•Energy. By giving your body a better and more reliable energy source, you will feel more energized during the day. Fats are shown to be the most effective molecule to burn as fuel.
•Hunger. Fat is naturally more satisfying and ends up leaving us in a satiated ("full") state for longer.
•Acne. Recent studies have shown a drop in acne lesions and skin inflammation over 12 weeks.

Ketogenic Holiday Recipes

Ketogenic Holiday Appetizers

Ketogenic Homemade Dill Dip

INGREDIENTS:

1 cup reduced fat sour cream
1/2 cup reduced fat mayonnaise
2 Tbsps. finely chopped Vidalia onion
2 Tbsps. finely chopped fresh Italian parsley
1 Tbsp. finely chopped dill weed
1 tsp. seasoned salt
freshly ground pepper to taste

INSTRUCTIONS:

Combine all ingredients in a medium bowl
Season to taste with salt and pepper
Refrigerate until well chilled

Ketogenic Apricot Coconut Shrimp

INGREDIENTS:

1 Cup Unsweetened Coconut Flakes
1 lb. Shrimp, peeled and deveined
2 large Egg Whites
2 Tbsp. Coconut Flour

Sweet Chili Dipping Sauce

1 Tbsp. Lime Juice
1 medium Red Chili, diced
1/2 Cup Sugar Free Apricot Preserves
1 1/2 Tbsp. Rive Wine Vinegar
1/4 tsp. Red Pepper Flakes

INSTRUCTIONS:

•Pre-heat your oven to 400 degrees Fahrenheit.
•Beat egg whites to produce soft peaks, and set out coconut flour and coconut flakes in separate bowls.
•First dip the shrimp in coconut flour, then in the egg white mixture, and lastly in the coconut flakes. Prepare a baking sheet greased with silpat and lay the shrimps flat on it.
•Cook the shrimp for fifteen minutes, turn and then broil for three to five more minutes or until the shrimp becomes brown on both sides.
•As you cook the shrimp, prepare the sauce. Mix thoroughly all the dipping sauce ingredients.
•Serve the shrimps with sauce on top.

NUTRITIONAL VALUE:

Calories	397
Carbs	6.5g
Fats	20g
Protein	36.5g

Ketogenic Devilish Eggs

INGREDIENTS:

12 large eggs
1/2 cup mayonnaise
2 Tbsps. of melted butter
1/2 tsp. yellow mustard
1/4 cup finely minced white onion
1/2 tsp. white pepper
1 tsp. salt

INSTRUCTIONS:

•Put the eggs in a large pot filled with cold water, heat it to boiling and let it cook for ten minutes
•Remove the pot from the heat and let it sit for another 3 minutes (pour out as much of the hot water as you can, without dumping the eggs out, then add cold water)
•Let the eggs stay in the cold water for between 5-10 minutes
•Remove the eggs, pat them dry and peel them
•After peeling, use a long, thin knife to cut the eggs lengthwise
•Remove the cooked yolks and set them in a separate glass bowl
•Place the white shells on a plate or a deviled egg holder and set aside
•Use a fork to break up the yolks until they are finely crumbled
•To the crumbled yolks, add the mayonnaise and the other ingredients, and mix them well (you may taste and adjust seasoning to your liking)
•Use a tsp. to fill the egg white cavities with the yolk mixture
(Tip: fill the cavities just up to the edge, you can add more of the mixture later if you will have enough left, this will ensure that you have each white eggshell filled)
Cover and refrigerate until ready to serve

5-Layer Keto Dip

INGREDIENTS:

20 Oz Guacamole

4 Oz Cream cheese

4 Oz Mayonnaise

8 Oz Sour Cream

2 Tbsps. Taco Seasoning

16 Oz Salsa

10 Oz Cheddar Cheese, Shredded

4 Oz Green Onions, Diced

INSTRUCTIONS:

- Begin by mixing the cream cheese, sour cream, mayonnaise and seasoning until you obtain a smooth mixture
- Chop the green onions
- Use a medium sized casserole dish to spread out the guacamole at the bottom, this will form the first layer
- Take the sour cream mixture and spread it carefully on top of the guacamole to form the second layer
- Then spread the salsa over the sour cream mixture, this should form the third layer
- Add the cheese evenly to form the fourth layer
- Lastly, spread the green onions on top
- (It is best served if let to stay in the refrigerator for between 1-24 hours to give adequate time for the flavors to blend well)

Keto Grilled Halloumi With Salsa

INGREDIENTS:

2 packages Halloumi cheese
1 cup strawberries
½ large cucumber
1 jalapeño pepper
juice from 1 lime
1 clove garlic
1 Tbsp. mint, chopped
2 Tbsp. basil, chopped
2 Tbsp. extra virgin olive oil
1 Tbsp. balsamic vinegar
1 Tbsp. ghee or butter
¼ tsp. salt or more to taste
freshly ground black pepper

INSTRUCTIONS:

- Peel and chop the cucumber and chop the strawberries.
- Deseed and thinly slice the jalapeño pepper.
- Chop the herbs, peel and mash the garlic and mix with the extra virgin olive oil, balsamic vinegar and fresh lime juice.
- In a bowl add everything together and season with salt and pepper and set aside.
- Slice the Halloumi cheese into about ½ inch / 1 cm slices and cook on both sides on a skillet greased with ghee or butter. You can use a regular or grill skillet like I did. Cook for 2-3 minutes on each side. Do not turn before the side gets brown and crispy.
- Place on a serving plate and top with the strawberry

Ketogenic Side Dishes

Keto Roasted Brussels Sprouts And Prosciutto Bites

INGREDIENTS:

1 lbs. small Brussels sprouts, rinsed of any dirt
2 Tbsps. extra-virgin olive oil
1/4 lbs. thinly sliced prosciutto
1 pinch coarse salt and freshly ground pepper

INSTRUCTIONS:

•Preheat the oven to 400F
•Slice the Brussels sprouts into half, lengthwise (do not trim the ends as they will hold together better with them)
•Toss the sprouts on a rimmed baking sheet with oil and sprinkle with salt and pepper

•Bake for up to 40 minutes, but begin checking at around the 25th minute mark, you can toss them around too
•Chop the prosciutto into small chunks
•Heat a medium-sized skillet over medium to high heat
•Add the prosciutto and sauté for about 5 minutes, or until nice and crispy, then set aside
•Remove the sprouts from the oven and allow them to cool for about 5 minutes, or until you can handle them
•Use a toothpick to slide on a sprout into two halves, followed by a slice or 3 of the ham, then bookend it with another sprout half
•Continue this way until you have about 32 mini skewers.
•Arrange on a platter and serve immediately

Ketogenic Cheesy Spinach

INGREDIENTS:

8 oz. Spinach
4 Tbsp. Cream Cheese
2 oz. shredded Cheddar Cheese

INSTRUCTIONS:

•Over medium heat, thaw the spinach
•Cook until it is completely thawed and the juices has reduced
•Add the cream cheese, mix thoroughly
•Add the cheddar cheese and mix well.
•Serve.

NUTRITIONAL VALUE:

Calories	230
Carbs	8g
Fats	19g
Protein	13g

Ketogenic Italian Spaghetti Squash

INGREDIENTS:

1 Cup marinara sauce
1 Cup shredded mozzarella cheese
1 lb. prepared meatballs
olive oil
2 medium-sized spaghetti squash
salt & pepper

INSTRUCTIONS:

•Pre-heat your oven at 400 degrees Fahrenheit.
•At the center of the spaghetti squash pierce several times on all sides using a sharp knife then put in the microwave for 3 mins. turn once.
•Cut the spaghetti squash in half lengthwise using a sharp knife then spoon out the seeds.
•On a foil-lined, non-stick baking sheet brush oil and then lay the spaghetti squash, season with pepper and salt.
•Roast for fifty and sixty mins., or until it is easy to insert the knife without resistance. Allow it to cool down for ten mins.
•While waiting for the squash to roast, prepare and cook the meatballs.
•If the squash is cool enough to handle, scrape the flesh using a fork to loosen and shake strands.
•Place 4 meatballs on top, ¼ cup shredded mozzarella cheese and ¼ cup sauce each, then broil until the cheese has turned into golden brown and becomes bubbly.

NUTRITIONAL VALUE:

Calories	253
Carbs	14.5g
Fats	11.3g
Protein	24.2g

Keto Chipotle Jicama Hash

INGREDIENTS:

4 slices bacon, chopped coarsely

12 oz. *jicama,* peeled and diced small

4 oz. purple onion, chopped

1 oz. green bell pepper (or *poblano*), seeded & chopped

4 Tbsp. my *Chipotle* Mayonnaise

INSTRUCTIONS:

•Using a non-stick skillet, brown the bacon over high heat

•Remove solid to paper toweling to drain

•Use the remaining bacon grease to stir fry the onions and jicama until the onion is tender and brown, and the jicama is brown as well and somewhat crunchy

•When almost ready, add the bell pepper and cook the hash until the bell pepper is tender

•Transfer the hash onto two plates and serve each plate dabbed with 2 Tbsp. Chipotle mayonnaise (If more mayo is needed, recalculate the figures above to include the additional mayo)

Keto Cauliflower Casserole

INGREDIENTS:

2 lb. raw cauliflower, trimmed of leaves and lower stalk
4 oz. chopped white onion
1 Tbsp. butter
2 oz. chicken broth
4 oz. heavy cream
4 oz. cream cheese
2 cups shredded Colby jack or cheddar

INSTRUCTIONS:

•Cut the cauliflower into small pieces, including the core
•Heat a large pan of lightly salted water to boil
•Add the cauliflower and cook over medium heat until completely tender (in case you have a steaming pan combo set, it would be advisable that you steam the cauliflower instead of boiling)
•Use a colander to drain the cauliflower, and set them aside
•Set the heat to medium, then use a large skillet to melt the butter and sauté the onions until soft and translucent
•Add all the cauliflower and use a spatula to break them into smaller pieces while mixing them with the onions
•Further reduce the heat to medium low and add the chicken broth and heavy cream while stirring
•Add cream cheese and stir until the cheese melts (you can add a little chicken broth if the mixture appears to be too thick)
•Lastly, add shredded cheese and stir until it melts and a creamy source is created
(You can choose to turn it into a baking dish and cover with more cheese, then bake for 15-20 minutes at 325F, or just serve and enjoy)

Ketogenic Slow Cooker Chicken Lettuce Wraps

INGREDIENTS:

3 large boneless skinless chicken breasts
1 celery stalk
1 onion, diced
1 clove garlic
16 oz. low sodium chicken broth
1/2 cup hot wing sauce
large lettuce leaves (Bibb or iceberg)
1 1/2 cups shredded carrots
2 large celery stalks, thinly sliced
blue cheese, for serving
ranch dressing, for serving

INSTRUCTIONS:

•Place the chicken breasts, celery stalk, diced onion and garlic in a slow cooker.
•Pour the chicken broth over the ingredients into the slow cooker.
•Place lid, cover and leave for 8 hours on low or 4 hours on high.
•Transfer the chicken breasts on to a platter.
•Takeout about ½ cup broth from the slow cooker and remove the balance broth.
•Use a fork to shred the meat and place back again into the slow cooker.
•Add the kept aside broth, sauce and cook for another 30 minutes.
•Serve the meat on lettuce wraps, topped up with the rest of the ingredients.
•If required serve with ranch dressing.

Keto Slow Cooker Cheese & Mushroom

Makes: 4 servings

INGREDIENTS:

2 (8 ounce) fresh mushrooms
½ cup butter, melted
1 ounce ranch dressing mix (hidden valley, 1 package)
2 tablespoons parmesan cheese, as much as desired

INSTRUCTION:

•Put mushrooms in the slow cooker.
•Add Ranch dressing to melted butter in a bowl.
•Mix and pour over mushrooms.
•Sprinkle with Parmesan Cheese.
•Cook for 4 hours on low.

Keto Slow Cooker Lentil Soup

Makes: 6 servings

INGREDIENTS:

8 oz. lentils, about 1 cup

12 to 16 oz. smoked sausage thinly sliced

2 cups chicken broth

1 large onion, diced

1 cup diced carrots

1/2 cup diced celery

2 cloves garlic, minced

1 can (14.5 oz.) diced tomatoes, un-drained

1 teaspoon salt

INSTRUCTIONS:

•Mix the lentils with sausage, chicken broth, onion, carrots, celery, and garlic in slow cooker.

•Cover and cook until tender on LOW for 5 to 6 hours.

•Cook for another 1 – 2 hours after tomatoes and salt are added.

Keto Slow Cooker Cabbage Tomato Chicken & Sausage Soup
Makes: 6-8 servings

INGREDIENTS:

6 cups chopped cabbage (1 lb.)
1 onion, chopped small
1 cup celery, diced small
2 cans (14.5 oz.) petite dice tomatoes
6 cups beef stock
2 tsp. dried thyme
1 tsp. ground fennel
fresh ground black pepper to taste
4 (or 6) links Sabatinos Chicken Sausage with Mozzarella, Artichokes and Garlic
2 tsp. olive oil
Freshly-grated Parmesan cheese for serving (optional)

INSTRUCTIONS:

•Chop cabbage, onion, and celery & put in the slow cooker
•Pour in the 2 cans of tomatoes, beef stock, dried thyme, ground fennel, and black •pepper to the slow cooker.
•Cook for 8-9 hours on low or 3-4 hours on high.
•Slice the sausage into ¼ inch pieces.
•Heat the olive oil over medium-high heat.
•Add sausage & cook until well browned.
•Stir in the sausage to the soup.
•Cook for 30-45 minutes on high.
•Serve with freshly-grated Parmesan cheese if desired.

Keto Slow Cooker Split Pea Soup
Makes: 8 servings

INGREDIENTS:

1 (16 oz.) pkg. dried green split peas, rinsed

1 meaty hambone, 2 ham hocks, or 2 cups diced ham

3 carrots, peeled and sliced

1/2 cup chopped onion

2 ribs of celery plus leaves, chopped

1 or 2 cloves of garlic, minced

1 bay leaf

1/4 cup fresh parsley, chopped, or 2 teaspoons dried parsley flakes

1 tbsp. seasoned salt (or to taste)

1/2 tsp. fresh pepper

1 1/2 qts. hot water

INSTRUCTIONS:

•Layer the ingredients in slow cooker in the above order.

•Pour in water.

•Do not stir.

•Cover and cook for 4 to 5 hours on high.

•Remove bones and bay leaf.

•Mash peas to thicken more.

•Garnish & serve with croutons. .

Keto Slow Cooker Seafood Soup
Makes: 8 – 10 servings

INGREDIENTS:

4 (6 1/2 oz.) cans minced clams with juice
1/2 lb. salt pork or bacon, diced
1 cup chopped onion
6 to 8 medium potatoes, peeled and cubed
3 cups water
3 1/2 teaspoons salt
1/4 teaspoon pepper
4 cups half and half cream or milk
3 to 4 tbsp. cornstarch
chopped fresh parsley, for garnish

INSTRUCTIONS:

•Chop clams into bite-sized pieces if necessary.
•Sauté salt pork or bacon and onion until golden brown & drain.
•Place in slow cooker with clams.
•Put in all remaining ingredients, except milk, cornstarch, and parsley.
•Cover and cook on high 3 to 4 hours until vegetables are tender.
•Mix 1 cup of milk or cream with the cornstarch
•Stir in cornstarch mixture and the remaining milk or cream during last hour of cooking..
•Top each serving with chopped parsley.
•Serve with crackers or crusty French bread

Keto Slow Cooker Chorizo & Chicken Soup

Makes: 8 servings

Per serving: Calories: 659, Fat: 47, Carbohydrates: 6, Fiber: 1, Protein: 52

INGREDIENTS:

4 lbs. Boneless Skinless Chicken Thighs
1 lb. Chorizo
4 Cups Chicken Stock
1 Cup Heavy Cream
1 Can Stewed Tomatoes
2 Tbsp. Minced Garlic
2 Tbsp. Worcestershire Sauce
2 Tbsp. Frank's Red Hot Sauce
Garnish with Shaved Parmesan and Sour Cream

INSTRUCTIONS:

•Brown the chorizo in skillet.
•Layer the ingredients in slow cooker.
•Start with the Chicken Thighs (raw), Chorizo then the remaining ingredients
•Cook on high for 3 hours
•Break up thighs apart, and return to slow cooker
•Cook for 30 more minutes on low
•Garnish with Shaved Parmesan and Sour Cream!

Ketogenic Slow Cooker Dinner Recipes

Keto Slow Cooker Lemongrass Pork
Makes: 6 – 8 servings

INGREDIENTS:

- 2-3 lbs. Pork Loin or Butt Roast
- 2 inch ginger
- 2-3 cloves garlic
- 2 tsp. kosher salt
- 3 TBS olive oil
- 3 TBS minced lemongrass
- 1 TBS apple cider vinegar
- 1 tsp. ground pepper
- 1 onion
- ½ can coconut milk

INSTRUCTIONS:

- Trim off any excess fat from the roast,
- Leave just a little.
- Slice a crisscross pattern into top fatty layer of the pork.
- Peel & mince the garlic.
- Peel & slice ginger into ¼ inch thick slices.
- Slice onion into ¼ inch rounds
- Put the onion rounds at the bottom of the slow cooker.
- Mix into a loose paste the olive oil, salt, minced garlic, minced lemongrass, apple cider vinegar, ground pepper.
- Apply the paste over the pork & place in slow cooker.
- Marinate covered, over night.
- Add ½ can of coconut milk to slow cooker the next day.
- Cook on low for 8 hours.
- When done, pork should fall apart.
- Shred with fork and serve!

Keto Slow Cooker Turkey Drumsticks

Makes: 4 servings

INGREDIENTS:

1 tablespoon olive oil
3 turkey drumsticks
Sprinkles salt and cracked black pepper, to taste
1 large Vidalia onion, chopped
3 large carrots, peeled and sliced into thin coins
2 large cloves garlic, minced
½ teaspoon dried sage, crumbled
2 tablespoons fresh parsley, chopped
1 tablespoon fresh thyme, chopped (or use 1 teaspoon dried)
1 lemon, halved

INSTRUCTIONS:

•Oil the bottom of the slow cooker with olive oil.
•Rub the drumsticks with olive oil.
•Season well with salt and pepper.
•Arrange the onions and carrots in the bottom of the cooker.
•Place the drumsticks over.
•Mix garlic, sage, parsley & thyme together.
•Sprinkle over the drumsticks.
•Squeeze the lemon halves gently to release juices into the vegetables.
•Let them nestle at the bottom of the pot.
•Cook for 8-10 hours on low, or high for 4-5 hours until meat is cooked through.

Keto Slow Cooker Pork with Apple & Mustard Sauce
Makes: 4 servings

INGREDIENTS:

2 lbs. pork shoulder joint
salt
1 cooking apple
4 oz. chicken/vegetable stock
½ tsp. Dijon mustard
½ tsp. English mustard
1 tsp. cumin/cinnamon

INSTRUCTIONS:

Apple sauce
•Core and peel the apple & chop it up.
•Put it in a bowl & sprinkle with a teaspoon of stevia, & a pinch of cumin r cinnamon.
•Add a few teaspoons of water and cover with cling film.
•Microwave for 2 minutes.
•Stir & repeat until the sauce is formed.
•Mix in mustard with the apple sauce.
•Stir the apple/mustard sauce with the stock.
•Trim the fat off the pork & place on a clean surface.
•Make a few slits in the pork to let all the juices in.
•Sprinkle salt and rub it in.
•Place pork in slow cooker
•Pour the apple / mustard sauce over.
•Cook on high for two hours.
•Turn heat to low and cook for another 4-8 hours.
•Remove the pork and slice as desired.
•Pour sauce over.

Keto Slow Cooker Meatloaf
Makes: 4 servings

INGREDIENTS:

Olive oil in a spritzer bottle, or non-stick cooking spray
2 lbs. extra lean ground sirloin
2 large eggs
1 cup (about 1 medium size) zucchini, grated and excess liquid squeezed out
1/2 cup freshly grated Parmesan cheese
1/2 cup fresh parsley, finely chopped, plus extra for garnish
4 cloves freshly minced garlic
3 Tablespoons balsamic vinegar
1 Tablespoon dried oregano
2 Tablespoons minced dry onion or onion powder
1/2 teaspoon sea or Kosher salt
1/2 teaspoon ground black pepper

TOPPING
1/4 cup ketchup or tomato sauce
1/4 cup shredded or 2-3 slices mozzarella cheese
2 Tablespoons fresh parsley chopped

INSTRUCTIONS:

•Line a large slow cooker with strips of aluminum foil.
•Spray with olive oil or non-stick cooking spray.
•Mix all ingredients except for cooking spray & topping ingredients.
•Pour mixture into the slow cooker.
•Shape into shaped of loaf a top of the aluminum foil strips.
•Put lid on top of slow cooker.
•Cook for 3 hours on high.
•Turn off the cooker 15 minutes before the end of cooking time.
•Take off lid
•Drizzle ketchup over the top of meatloaf.
•Top with cheese & replace the lid of slow cooker.
•Leave for 5-10 minutes until cheese melts.
•Transfer to serving platter & garnish with fresh parsley.

Keto Slow Cooker Chicken & Garlic Butter

Makes: 4 – 6 servings

INGREDIENTS:

For the garlic chicken
2- 2.5 lbs. of chicken breasts
1 stick of butter
8 garlic cloves, sliced in half to release flavor
1.5 tsp. salt
Optional -- 1 sliced onion
<u>Cheese sauce</u>
8 oz. of cream cheese
1 cup of chicken stock (I use the liquid left in the slow cooker after the chicken is removed.)
salt to taste

INSTRUCTIONS:

•Place the chicken in slow cooker.
•Put in the butter.
•Add the garlic spreading it around evenly.
•Sprinkle salt.
•Cover & cook on low for 6 hours.
•When done take out & place on serving platter.

Cheese sauce
•Pour cup of chicken stock into a pan (or liquid from the slow cooker).
•Stir in the cream cheese and salt.
•Cook until sauce is well blended & creamy over low medium heat.
•When done, pour over chicken.

Keto Slow Cooker Lime Chicken

Makes: 1 serving

INGREDIENTS:

24-oz. jar medium salsa
Juice from one lime
1/4 cup fresh cilantro, chopped
1.25-oz. package taco seasoning
2 jalapeños peppers, finely chopped (optional)
6 boneless chicken breast halves

INSTRUCTIONS:

•Mix together salsa, lime juice, cilantro, taco seasoning and jalapenos in slow cooker.
•Put in the chicken and coat with the salsa mixture.
•Cook covered, for 6 hours on low setting.
•Spoon salsa mixture over top.

Keto Slow Cooker Pot Roast
Makes: 6 – 8 servings

INGREDIENTS:

5 lb. pot roast
Himalayan Salt (or similar)
2 tablespoons tallow or lard
3 cups bone broth

INSTRUCTIONS:

•Salt the Roast generously.
•Heat the fat on medium-high heat.
•Brown the roast on all sides .
•Place in the slow cooker.
•Deglaze pan with the bone broth.
•Pour over the roast.
•Cook for 7-8 hours on low.

Keto Slow Cooker Chicken Drumsticks

Makes: 12 servings

Per serving: 587 calories, 42.8g fat, 640mg sodium, 0.7g carb, 53.5g protein

INGREDIENTS:

1/2 cup liquid aminos (or gluten free soy sauce)
2 cups water
1 teaspoon ground ginger
1 teaspoon garlic powder
2 tablespoons sweetener
1/4 teaspoon blackstrap molasses (optional)
6 1/2 lbs. chicken, cut into pieces
Salt and pepper

INSTRUCTIONS:

•Mix together soy aminos, water, ground ginger, garlic powder, sweetener, and molasses in slow cooker.
•Season chicken with salt and pepper.
•Add chicken to slow cooker.
•Cook for 5 – 6 hours on high.

Keto Slow Cooker Chuck Roast

Makes: 4 – 6 servings

INGREDIENTS:

3-4 lb. beef chuck roast
2 cups beef stock
2 tbsp. red wine vinegar
2 tbsp. Worcestershire sauce
¼ cup soy sauce
1 tbsp. tomato paste
1 tbsp. liquid smoke
1 tsp. garlic powder
1 tsp. onion powder
Provolone cheese (optional)
Salt and pepper to taste

INSTRUCTIONS:

•Mix all of the ingredients together.
•Place in slow cooker.
•Lastly add the chuck roast.
•Cook on high for 4 hours

Ketogenic Holiday Dinner Recipes

Ketogenic Glazed Duck Breast

INGREDIENTS:

1 6 oz. Duck Breast
1 Cup Spinach
1 Tbsp. Heavy Cream
1 Tbsp. Swerve Sweetener
1/2 tsp. Orange Extract
1/4 tsp. Sage
2 Tbsp. Butter

INSTRUCTIONS:

•Score the duck breast skin on top.
•Season it with pepper and salt.
•Heat a pan over med-low heat, add butter and move the pan. Cook the butter until is slightly browned.
•Add orange extract and sage in the browned butter. Cook until the butter becomes deep amber in color
•While waiting, place the duck breast in a cold pan. Place the pans on the stove with med-high heat.
•After few mins. turn the duck breast and check the crispy skin.
•Add heavy cream in the orange and sage butter mixture, then stir well. Pour it over the duck breast and mix it with the duck fat. Continue cooking for another 5 to 10 mins.
•In the pan you used to make the sauce, wilt the spinach.
•Allow the duck to rest for two to three minutes, then slice and place the wilted spinach with sauce on top.

NUTRITIONAL VALUE:

Calories	798
Carbs	1g
Fats	71g
Protein	36g

Ketogenic Ribeye Steak Dinner

INGREDIENTS:

1 Tbsp. Butter
1 Tbsp. Duck Fat
1/2 tsp. chopped Thyme
16 oz. Ribeye Steak (1 – 1 1/4 inch thick)
Salt and Pepper to Taste

INSTRUCTIONS:

•Pre-heat your oven to 400 degrees Fahrenheit. Place the cast iron skillet in your oven and heat it.
•Prepare your steak by putting oil or duck fat. Then put enough amount of salt and pepper on all sides and the edges.
•Remove the cast iron skillet from the oven and place on the stove with medium heat. Add the oil or duck fat and put the steak in the pan and sear. Do the searing for 1 ½ to two minutes.
•Turn the steak and place it in the oven right away for four to six minutes. Don't panic if it produces some smoke, it will cool down slightly and the smoke will stop.
•Measure ½ tsp. chopped thyme and 2 Tbsp. butter.
•Remove the steak from the oven and place it in the stove with low heat. Place the butter in the pan and use butter to base the steak. Push the cast iron handle downward and collect the butter using a spoon, ladle it over the steak. Continue doing this for two to four minutes until you achieve the desired doneness.
•Place the cover, and allow it to rest for five minutes.
•Serve together with your favorite vegetables and additional butter if you want.

NUTRITIONAL VALUE:

Calories	749.5
Carbs	0
Fats	66g
Protein	38g

Ketogenic Ancho Chili Powder Turkey Legs

INGREDIENTS:

1 tsp. Liquid Smoke
1 tsp. Worcestershire
half tsp. Ancho Chili Powder
2 tsp. Salt
1/4 tsp. Cayenne Pepper
half tsp. Dried Thyme
2 medium Turkey Legs
half tsp. Garlic Powder
2 Tbsp. Duck Fat
half tsp. Onion Powder
half tsp. Pepper

INSTRUCTIONS:

•In a small bowl place all the dry spices. Then add the liquid ingredients and combine together.
•Use paper towels to pat the turkey legs dry. Then rub the seasoning in the turkey's legs.
•Preheat your oven to 350 degrees Fahrenheit. In a cast iron skillet, heat two Tbsp. of fat. •Add the turkey legs, as soon as the oil starts to smoke and sear for around one to two minutes on each side. Make sure that you sear the entire leg.
•Place the turkey legs in the oven and bake for one hour or until cooked through.
•Take the turkey out of the oven and allow it to rest for a few minutes.
•Serve together with your favorite side dish and enjoy.

NUTRITIONAL VALUE:

Calories   382
Carbs   0.8g
Fats   22.5g
Protein   44g

Ketogenic Curry Chicken Thighs

INGREDIENTS:

1 1/2 tsp. Salt

1 tsp. Garlic Powder

1 tsp. Ground Cumin

1 tsp. Paprika

1/2 tsp. Allspice

1/2 tsp. Cayenne Pepper

1/2 tsp. Chili Powder

1/2 tsp. Ground Coriander

1/4 C. Olive Oil

1/4 tsp. Ginger

1/4 tsp. Ground Cardamom

1/4 tsp. Ground Cinnamon

2 tsp. Yellow Curry

8 Bone-In, Skin-On Chicken Thighs

INSTRUCTIONS:

•Pre-heat your oven to 425 degrees Fahrenheit.

•Combine all the ingredients in the bowl.

•Lay all the 8 chicken thighs on a baking sheet and wrap it with a foil.

•Rub all chicken thighs with olive oil.

•Rub the spice mixture on both sides of the chicken, coating entirely.

•Bake for fifty minutes.

•Before serving allow it to cool down.

NUTRITIONAL VALUE:

Calories	277
Carbs	0.6g
Fats	19.9g
Protein	21.1g

Ketogenic Grilled Cilantro Beef

INGREDIENTS:

¼ Cup fresh minced cilantro

¼ tsp. cumin

½ tsp. coriander

1 large chopped shallot

1 tsp. coconut sugar (optional)

1 tsp. red pepper flakes

1/4 Cup extra virgin olive oil

2 lb. chuck roast

2 tsp. oregano

2 tsp. sea salt

4 cloves minced garlic

juice of 1 orange

juice of 2 limes

INSTRUCTIONS:

•Wash the chuck roast with cold water and then wipe it dry. Put aside and allow it to stand for thirty minutes.

•In your food processor, place all the ingredients and blend to combine.

•In a slow cooker, place chuck roast and coat it with asada marinade.

•Add filtered water in the slow cooker – this enables the meat to heat up evenly instead of scorching it in the slow cooker. Cook for five hours on high and turn meat every hour.

•Take the chuck out from the slow cooker and allow it to rest for twenty minutes.

•Slice the meat and pour the juices from the slow cooker.

•Serve and enjoy.

NUTRITIONAL VALUE:

Calories	183
Carbs	116g
Fats	56g
Protein	208g

Ketogenic Peppered Baked Beef

INGREDIENTS:

1 1/4 Cup plain yogurt, beaten lightly
1 tbsp. paprika
1/2 tbsp. pepper
1/2 tsp. cayenne
1/2 tsp. ginger
2 lbs. beef stew meat
2 tsps. salt
3 minced onions
6 garlic cloves
6 Tbsps. vegetable oil

INSTRUCTIONS:

•Pre-heat your oven to 350 degrees Fahrenheit. In a huge stockpot, heat the oil over med-high heat. Add the beef and cook until golden brown.
•Remove the browned beef and put in a bowl to collect the juices.
•Add garlic and onions to pot and then sauté until brown. Place the browned meat and the juices in the pot again. Add in cayenne, salt, pepper, ginger and paprika. Add the yogurt and then simmer.
•Use aluminum foil to cover the pot and replace the lid. Bake for 1 ½ hour. if needed, add water before baking to make sure the meat remains tender.

NUTRITIONAL VALUE:

Calories	264
Carbs	10g
Fats	151.2
Proteins	271.2g

Ketogenic Roasted Chicken with Squash Pasta

INGREDIENTS:

1 cracks black pepper
1 small spaghetti squash
1 tsp. garlic salt
1/2 tsp. cayenne pepper
2 Cup heavy cream
2 Tbsp. Cajun seasoning + 1tsp
3 Tbsp. butter
4 small chicken breasts

INSTRUCTIONS:

•Create holes in your spaghetti squash and put it in a microwave for 15mins.
•Once the spaghetti is done, cut it into half. Remove and discard the seeds.
•Scoop out the squash noodles with a metal spoon, the noodles should come out easily. Put aside.
•Prepare your chicken by pounding and tenderizing it until it is about one inch tall and flat.
•Season your chicken by adding 2 Tbsp. of Cajun seasoning and coat.
•In a big pan over medium heat, heat some olive oil.
•Add the chicken covered with seasoning. Turn after five to ten minutes.
•Meanwhile heat up butter, one tsp. seasoning, cream, ½ tsp. cayenne pepper and garlic salt in a separate medium-sized pan with medium heat.
•When it starts to boil, add the squash and simmer over medium low to reduce.
•The sauce should reduce half over for 20 mins. as your chicken cooks.
•The chicken should turns into brown but not burn. If the chicken reaches the temperature of 180 degrees Fahrenheit, take it out of the pan and allow it to rest for five minutes.

•Turn off the heat in your noodle. Make sure that the sauce will not stick to squash but there should be some liquid remaining. Allow the chicken breasts to rest.
•Cut the chicken diagonally.
•Remove the noodles from the heat, arrange in the plate and add some dollop on top of each chicken breast.
•If you like you can sprinkle more Cajun seasoning.
•Serve.

NUTRITIONAL VALUE:

Calories	391
Carbs	37g
Fats	9.8g
Protein	37g

Ketogenic Citrusy Cheesecake

INGREDIENTS:

8 oz. cream cheese, softened
2 oz. heavy cream
1 tsp. Stevia Glycerite
1 tsp. (packet) Splenda or other powdered or liquid low carb sweetener
1 Tbsp. lemon juice
1 tsp. of vanilla flavoring

INSTRUCTIONS:

Mix together ingredients.
Whip until pudding consistency.
Put in cups.
Refrigerate.

Ketogenic Nutty Cookie Butter

INGREDIENTS:

1 cup Raw Macadamias
3/4 cup Raw Cashews
1 tsp. Vanilla
1/4 tsp. Cinnamon
1/4 tsp. Ginger
1/8 tsp. Nutmeg
1/8 tsp. Cloves
2 tbsp. Butter
2 tbsp. Heavy Cream
2 tbsp. Swerve, powdered
Pinch Salt

INSTRUCTIONS:

In a food processor, blend together macadamia nuts and cashews until smooth.
In a saucepan, begin to brown butter along with the Swerve.
Once browned, mix in heavy cream.
Remove from heat.
To nut mixture, add vanilla and spices, cream and butter.
Process again, ensuring no lumps.
Add in caramel sauce and process until desired consistency is reached.

Ketogenic Chocolate Chia Raspberry Pudding

INGREDIENTS:

3 Tbsps. Chia Seeds

1 cup Unsweetened Almond Milk

1 scoop Chocolate Protein Powder

1/4 cup Raspberries fresh or frozen

1 tsp. Optional : Honey

INSTRUCTIONS:

Mix together almond milk and protein powder.
Mix in chia seeds.
Let rest 5 minutes before stirring.
Refrigerate 30 minutes.
Top with raspberries.

Ketogenic Lemon Coconut Vanilla Dessert

INGREDIENTS:

½ cup extra virgin coconut oil, softened
½ cup coconut butter, softened
zest and juice of one lemon
seeds from ½ a vanilla bean

INSTRUCTIONS:

Whisk ingredients in an easy to pour cup.
Pour into lined cupcake or loaf pan.
Refrigerate 30 minutes.
Top with lemon zest.

Ketogenic Caramel Marble Brownies

INGREDIENTS:

2 cups Almond Flour

1/2 cup Unsweetened Cocoa Powder

1/3 cup Erythritol

1/4 cup Coconut Oil

1/4 cup Maple Syrup

2 large Eggs

1 tbsp. Psyllium Husk Powder

2 tbsp. Torani Salted Caramel

1 tsp. Baking Powder

1/2 tsp. Salt

INSTRUCTIONS:

Preheat oven to 350 degrees.

In a bowl, beat together wet ingredients.

To the wet ingredients, slowly beat in dry ingredients.

Bake in an 11x7 well-greased brownie pan for 20 minutes.

Ketogenic Extreme Frozen Dessert

INGREDIENTS:

½ cup extra virgin coconut oil

½ cup butter, grass-fed

6 large egg yolks, free range or organic

2 large egg whites, free-range or organic

¼ cup Erythritol

25-30 drops Stevia extract (Clear / Vanilla)

1 cup coconut milk

2 tbsp. home-made vanilla extract

INSTRUCTIONS:

Separate egg yolks and egg whites.

Soften butter and coconut oil.

Whip egg whites until they form soft peaks

Blend together, butter, coconut, vanilla, erythritol and Stevia.

Add in egg yolk, one at a time.

Blend until smooth.

Blend it coconut milk.

Incorporate egg whites.

Put mixture in ice-cream maker.

Halfway through, remove ice cream and blend.

Return to ice-cream maker.

Blend again if lumps are noticeable.

Ketogenic White Chocolate Berry Cheesecake

INGREDIENTS:

8 oz. cream cheese, softened
2 oz. heavy cream
1 tsp. Stevia Glycerite
1 tsp. low sugar raspberry preserves
1 Tbsp. Sugar Free Syrup, White Chocolate flavor

INSTRUCTIONS:

Whip together ingredients to a pudding consistency.
Put in cups.
Refrigerate.

etogenic Fall Spice Scone Cookies

_ɔ:

1 Sweet Lightning Winter Squash (or 1 1/4 cup Pumpkin Puree, strained)
2 tsp. Cinnamon
2 tsp. Garam Masala
1 tbsp. Coconut Oil Cooking Spray
2 large Eggs
1 tsp. Vanilla Extract
1 tsp. Baking Powder
1 cup Almond Flour
1/4 cup Butter
1/4 cup Pumpkin Pie Spice

INSTRUCTIONS:

Preheat oven to 400 degrees.
Remove flesh from squash.
Slice squash.
Spray with coconut oil.
Place on parchment paper
Season with cinnamon and garam marsala.
Bake until tender 30-35 minutes.
Remove and place in food processor and process along with other ingredients.
Bake at 350 degrees.

Ketogenic Coconut Dessert

INGREDIENTS:

1 Can unsweetened full fat coconut milk
Berries of choice
Dark chocolate (optional)

INSTRUCTIONS:

Refrigerate coconut milk 12-24 hours
Remove thickened coconut milk
Whip 2-3 minutes
Fold in berries
Garnish with chocolate shavings

togenic Chocolate Avocado Mousse
rS:

2 small very ripe avocados

1/4 cup water

3 Tbsps. cocoa

6 Tbsps. granular Splenda or equivalent liquid Splenda

1/2 tsp. vanilla

Pinch salt

INSTRUCTIONS:

In a food processor or blender, process ingredients for 4-5 minutes.
Chill.

Ketogenic Coconut Macaroons

INGREDIENTS:

4 large egg whites
1 tsp. vanilla
1/4 tsp. cream of tartar
1/8 tsp. salt
1 cup erythritol
16 oz. finely shredded, unsweetened dried coconut
8 oz. cream cheese, softened
2 oz. heavy cream
2 oz. Sugar Free White Chocolate Syrup
2 oz. Semi-Sweet Mini Chocolate Chips

INSTRUCTIONS:

Preheat oven to 325 degrees.
Line 2 large baking sheets with parchment paper.
In a large mixing bowl, on low, beat together egg whites, vanilla, cream of tartar and salt until soft peaks form.
Add erythritol a Tbsp. at a time.
Beat until stiff peaks form.
Fold in coconut.
Beat together cream cheese and cream until smooth.
Mix in syrup.
Add in coconut mixture, a little at a time.
Fold in chocolate chips.
Using a small ice cream scoop, place mixture on baking sheet.
Bake 20-25 minutes.
Turn off oven leaving cookies in for 30 minutes.
Move to wire rack.
Let cool.

Ketogenic Lemony Coconut Ice Cream

INGREDIENTS:

3 cups homemade coconut milk

1/4 cup chia seeds

1/3 cup lemon juice, freshly squeezed

1/2 cup honey

1/4 cup coconut oil or ghee, melted

3 Tbsp. poppy seeds

INSTRUCTIONS:

Blend together all ingredients.

Chill.

Put in ice-cream maker.

Ketogenic Coffee Explosion

INGREDIENTS:

2 heaped tbsp. Flaxseed, ground

3 oz. cooking cream 35% fat

1 tsp. Cocoa powder, dark and unsweetened

1 tbsp. Goji berries

Freshly brewed coffee

Liquid sweetener, a couple of drops

INSTRUCTIONS:

Mix together flaxseeds, cream and cocoa, sweetener and coffee.

Garnish with Goji berries.

Ketogenic Crustless Chocolate Cheesecake

INGREDIENTS:

8 oz. cream cheese, softened

2 oz. heavy cream

1 tsp. Stevia Glycerite

1 tsp. (packet) Splenda or other powdered or liquid low carb sweetener

1 oz. Enjoy Life Mini chocolate chips

INSTRUCTIONS:

Whip together all ingredients except chocolate until a pudding consistency.

Fold in chocolate chips.

Refrigerate in serving cups.

Ketogenic Peanutty Frozen Dessert

INGREDIENTS:

1 Cup Cottage Cheese

1 Scoop Protein Powder

2 Tbsp. Peanut Butter

2 Tbsp. Heavy Cream

6 Drops Splenda

1 Hand blender or food processor

INSTRUCTIONS:

In a food processor, blend together ingredients except protein powder.

When smooth mix in protein powder, blend to remove chunks.

Freeze for 40 minutes.

Ketogenic Chocolate Roll Cake

INGREDIENTS:

1 cup Almond Flour

4 tbsp. Butter, melted

3 large Eggs

1/4 cup Psyllium Husk Powder

1/4 cup Cocoa Powder

1/4 cup Coconut Milk

1/4 cup Sour Cream

1/4 cup Erythritol

1 tsp. Vanilla

1 tsp. Baking Powder

Cream Cheese Filling:

8 oz. Cream Cheese

8 tbsp. Butter

1/4 cup Sour Cream

1/4 cup Erythritol

1/4 tsp. Stevia

1 tsp. Vanilla

INSTRUCTIONS:

Preheat oven to 350 degrees.

Stir together dry ingredients.

Slowly mix in wet ingredients.

Spread dough on a baking sheet.

Bake 12-15 minutes.

Mix together cream cheese filling.

Spread cream cheese filling over cake.

Roll tightly.

Ketogenic No Bake Cheesecake

INGREDIENTS:

8 oz. cream cheese, softened

2 oz. heavy cream

1 tsp. Stevia Glycerite

1 Tbsp. Dutch process cocoa powder

1 Tbsp. Sugar Free Syrup, Cherry flavor

3-5 drops EZSweet liquid Splenda

INSTRUCTIONS:

Whip together all ingredients except Ezsweet until a pudding consistency.

Sweeten to taste with Ezsweet.

Refrigerate in small cups.

Ketogenic Blackberry Cake

INGREDIENTS:

The Cake
1 1/2 cups Almond Flour
1/4 cup Erythritol, powdered
2 tbsp. Psyllium Husk Powder
1/2 cup Sour Cream
1/3 cup Salted Butter
2 large Eggs
1 1/2 tsp. Baking Powder
2 tbsp. Poppy Seeds
Zest of 1 Lemon
1 tsp. Vanilla Extract
1/4 tsp. Liquid Stevia

The Icing
2 tbsp. Lemon Juice
1/2 cup Erythritol, powdered
1/2 cup Blackberries, strained
1/4 cup Heavy Cream
6 tbsp. Butter

INSTRUCTIONS:

Preheat oven to 350 degrees.
Over medium low heat, brown butter.
Mix together all dry ingredients.
In separate bowl, mix together all wet ingredients.
Add brown butter to wet ingredients.
Slowly mix in dry ingredients to wet ingredients
Mix until dough forms.
Put dough into greased round cake pan.
Bake 20-25 minutes.
Let cool on cooling rack.

In a food processor, purée blackberries.
Strain.
Mix with lemon and erythritol.
Cream together, butter and heavy cream.
Mix into blackberry purée.
Ice the cake and refrigerate 20-30 minutes.

Ketogenic Peanut Butter Cookies

INGREDIENTS:

4 oz. cream cheese, softened

2 Tbsps. butter, room temperature

1 cup unsweetened natural peanut butter

2/3 cup powdered erythritol

1/2 cup Brown Just Like Sugar

1 tsp. stevia glycerite

5 drops EZSweet liquid Splenda

2 large eggs

2 tsps. pure vanilla extract

2 cups almond flour

1/8 tsp. xanthum gum

1/4 tsp. salt

1 tsp. baking soda

INSTRUCTIONS:

Preheat oven to 350 degrees.

Whisk together almond flour, xanthium gum, baking soda, and salt.

Line a baking sheet with parchment.

Mix together cream cheese, butter and peanut butter until smooth.

Add sweeteners and mix until fluffy.

Mix in one egg at a time.

Add Vanilla and flour mixture.

Mix well.

Roll in into balls 1 Tbsp. of dough.

Press lightly with fork.

Bake 10-12 minutes.

Ketogenic Dark Chocolate Peppermint Frozen Dessert

INGREDIENTS:

1 Cup Heavy Cream

½ Cup Light Cream

½ tsp. Liquid Stevia Extract

½ tsp. Vanilla (Optional)

Several Drops Peppermint Extract (Optional)

1 Square Dark Chocolate (Optional)

Several Drops Green food coloring (Optional)

INSTRUCTIONS:

Whisk together all ingredients except chocolate.

Freeze for 5 minutes.

Add to ice-cream maker.

Add shavings before ice cream has set.

Ketogenic Chocolate Avocado Ice Cream

INGREDIENTS:

2 ripe Hass Avocados
1 cup Coconut Milk
1/2 cup Heavy Cream
1/2 cup Cocoa Powder
2 tsp. Vanilla Extract
1/2 cup Erythritol, Powdered
25 drops Liquid Stevia
6 squares Unsweetened Baker's Chocolate

INSTRUCTIONS:

Scoop avocado into a bowl.
Add coconut milk, cream, and vanilla extract.
With an immersion blender, proceed to cream together.
Add Erythritol, stevia, and cocoa powder to the avocado mixture and mix well.
Add chop bakers chocolate.
Chill 6-12 hours, then about 20 minutes before you're ready to serve, add mixture to ice cream machine as per manufacturer's instructions.

Conclusion

Thank you again for downloading this book!

I hope this book was able to help you discover some amazing Keto Recipes.

The next step is to get cooking!!!

CPSIA information can be obtained
at www.ICGtesting.com
Printed in the USA
LVOW01s1546150616

492731LV00017B/657/P

9 781519 121318